# Famous Inventors & Inventions

Speedy Publishing LLC
40 E. Main St. #1156
Newark, DE 19711

www.speedypublishing.com

Copyright 2014
9781680321050
First Printed September 19, 2014

 speedypublishing

# Famous Inventions

# Famous Inventions

The inventors of the first airplane were Orville and Wilbur Wright. On December 17, 1903, the Wright brothers made the first successful experiment in which a machine carrying a man rose by its own power, flew naturally and at even speed, and descended without damage.

# Famous Inventions

The first ever elevator was designed to lift a passenger in 1743. This was made exclusively for King Louis in France. Though this looked nothing like elevators of today, it was called a flying chair.

# Famous Inventions

The Hall Braille typewriter was invented in 1892 by Frank Haven Hall.

# Famous Inventions

Alfred Bernhard Nobel invented many powerful and relatively safe explosives and explosive devices

# Famous Inventions

Karl Benz patented the three-wheeled Motor Car in 1886. It was the first true, modern automobile.

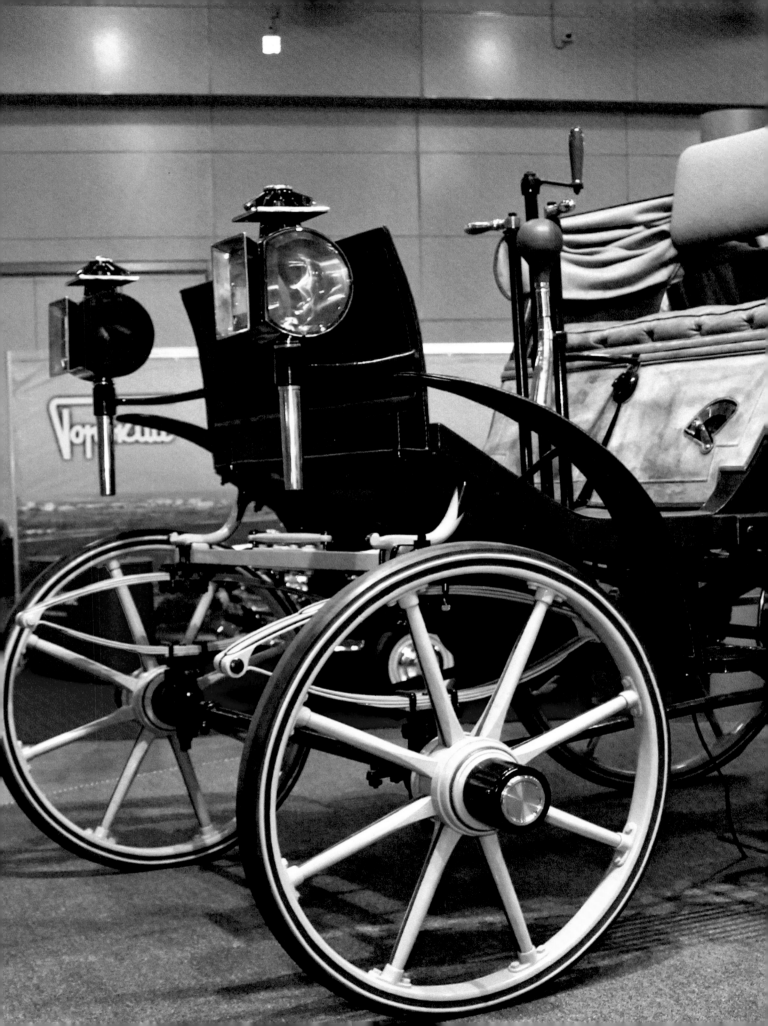

# Famous Inventions

Leonardo da Vinci had sketched a horseless, mechanized cart in the early 1500s. Like many of his designs, it wasn't built in his lifetime.

# Famous Inventions

Linus Yale, Jr. is best known for his inventions of locks, especially the cylinder lock.

# Famous Inventions

The telephone
In the 1870s, two inventors Elisha Gray and Alexander Graham Bell both independently designed devices that could transmit speech electrically.

# Famous Inventions

"Mr. Watson -- come here -- I want to see you." is the most famous first words uttered in the telephone by Mr. Alexander Graham Bell dated last March 10, 1876

# Famous Inventions

Alhazen (Ibn Al-Haytham) has a great authority on optics in the Middle Ages who lived around 1000AD, invented the first pinhole camera, also called the Camera Obscura

# Famous Inventions

On a summer day in 1827, Joseph Nicephore Niepce made the first photographic image with a camera obscura .

# Famous Inventions

The first typewriter was invented in 1867 by the American printer and editor Christopher Latham Sholes.

# Famous Inventions

Elisha Graves Otis invented the elevator brake, which greatly improved the safety of elevators. He used a ratchet on a spring to catch the elevator in the event of an accident.

# Famous Inventions

Louis Daguerre was the inventor of the first practical process of photography

The potato chip was invented in 1853 by George Crum.

# Famous Inventions

Thomas Alva Edison improved the incandescent electric light bulb.

# Famous Inventions

Thomas Alva Edison experimented with thousands of different light bulb filaments to find just the right materials to glow well, be long-lasting, and be inexpensive.

In 1877 the first phonograph was invented by Thomas Edison. The phonograph was the first method of recording and playing back sound.

# Famous Inventions

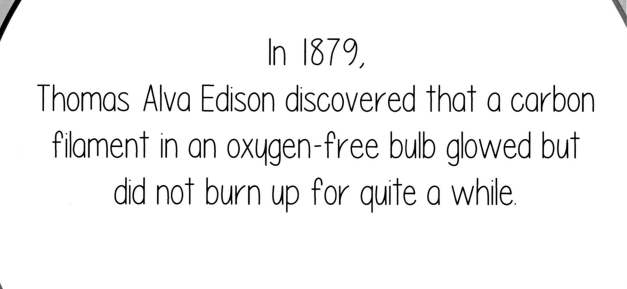

In 1879,
Thomas Alva Edison discovered that a carbon
filament in an oxygen-free bulb glowed but
did not burn up for quite a while.

# Famous Inventions

Emile Berliner came up with the Gramophone. He was the first inventor to stop recording on cylinders and start recording on flat discs or records.

# Famous Inventions

The laboratory Bunsen burner was invented by Robert Wilhelm Bunsen in 1855. Bunsen (1811-1899) was a German chemist and teacher. He invented the Bunsen burner for his research in isolating chemical substances - it has a high-intensity, non-luminous flame that does not interfere with the colored flame emitted by chemicals being tested.

# Famous Inventions

The game of basketball was invented by James Naismith. Naismith was a Canadian physical education instructor who invented the game in 1891 so that his students could participate in sports during the winter.

# Famous Inventions

Yale patented his cylinder pin-tumbler lock in 1861. This very secure lock is still widely in use today in car doors and the outside doors of buildings. The cylinder pin-tumbler lock consists of (usually 5) pairs of bottom pins and top drivers, held in position by springs. When the right key is put into the lock, the bottom pins are pushed to the right position, allowing the key to turn and the lock to unlock.

# CYLINDER PIN-TUMBLER LOCK

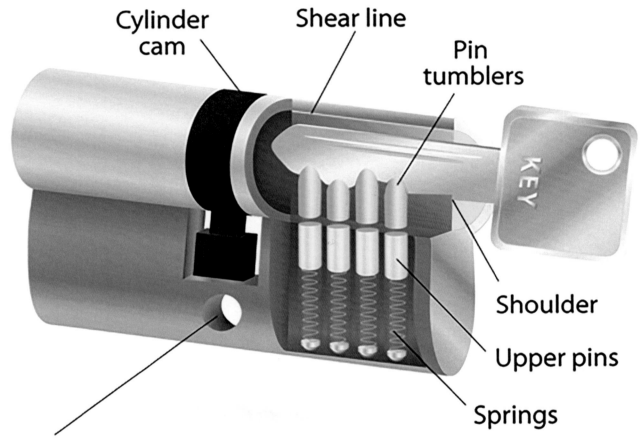

Cylinder cam

Shear line

Pin tumblers

Shoulder

Upper pins

Springs

Retaining screw hole

KEY

Made in the USA
San Bernardino, CA
05 May 2015